Civil Rights Crusaders

JESSE JACKSON

By Barbara M. Linde

Gareth Stevens
Publishing

Please visit our website, www.garethstevens.com. For a free color catalog of all our high-quality books, call toll free 1-800-542-2595 or fax 1-877-542-2596.

Library of Congress Cataloging-in-Publication Data

Linde, Barbara M.
Jesse Jackson / Barbara M. Linde.
    p. cm.—(Civil rights crusaders)
Includes index.
ISBN 978-1-4339-5684-3 (pbk.)
ISBN 978-1-4339-5685-0 (6-pack)
ISBN 978-1-4339-5682-9 (library binding)
1. Jackson, Jesse, 1941—Juvenile literature. 2. Civil rights workers—United States—Biography—Juvenile literature. 3. African Americans—Biography—Juvenile literature. 4. Presidential candidates—United States—Biography—Juvenile literature. I. Title.
E185.97.J25L56 2011
973.927092—dc22
[B]

2010050840

First Edition

Published in 2012 by
Gareth Stevens Publishing
111 East 14th Street, Suite 349
New York, NY 10003

Copyright © 2012 Gareth Stevens Publishing

Designer: Katelyn E. Reynolds
Editor: Kristen Rajczak

Photo credits: Cover, pp. 3–24, back cover (background) Shutterstock.com; cover, p. 1 Oli Scarff/Getty Images; p. 5 Jahi Chikwendiu/The Washington Post via Getty Images; p. 7 Michael Mauney/Time & Life Pictures/Getty Images; pp. 9, 11 Robert Abbott Sengstacke/Getty Images; p. 13 Andrew Cutraro/AFP/Getty Images; p. 15 David Hume Kennerly/Getty Images; p. 17 Scott Olson/Getty Images; p. 19 Spencer Platt/Getty Images.

Printed in the United States of America

CPSIA compliance information: Batch #CS11GS: For further information contact Gareth Stevens, New York, New York at 1-800-542-2595.

CONTENTS

Words in the glossary appear in **bold** type the first time they are used in the text.

CIVIL RIGHTS LEADER

Jesse Jackson is an important **civil rights** leader. He's also a Baptist **minister** and a **politician**. He has been fighting discrimination and segregation since the 1960s. Justice and equality are his goals. He believes in using peaceful methods to make changes. Jesse helps African Americans and other **minority groups**. He tells students to study and stay in school.

Everywhere he goes, Jesse tells people that they can do anything they set their minds to.

LET FREEDOM RING

"Discrimination" means treating people differently because of their race or beliefs. "Segregation" is the forced separation of people based on their race or class.

Jesse Jackson speaks to a crowd at a **protest** in 2010.

EARLY LIFE

Jesse Louis Jackson was born on October 8, 1941, in Greenville, South Carolina. He got good grades and played sports. He was the president of his high school class.

While in college, Jesse became part of the civil rights movement. He was a leader in a group that worked for racial equality. In 1964, Jesse graduated from a college in North Carolina. He soon moved to Chicago, Illinois, where he studied for the ministry. He became a Baptist minister in 1968.

LET FREEDOM RING

Jesse married Jacqueline Lavinia Brown in 1962. They raised five children together.

This photo shows Jesse walking his children to school in 1974.

▽

OPERATION BREADBASKET

Jesse had great respect for Martin Luther King Jr. In 1965, he joined Martin's Southern Christian Leadership Conference (SCLC). The SCLC ran Operation Breadbasket. It aided black workers and businesses. Jesse helped start the Chicago branch of Operation Breadbasket. Later, he became the national director. Under his direction, many black Americans got jobs. Businesses grew. However, Jesse and other SCLC leaders didn't always get along well. Jesse left the SCLC in 1971 and started his own group.

LET FREEDOM RING

Jesse was in Memphis, Tennessee, with Martin Luther King Jr. on the day Martin was shot and killed.

Just 4 days after Martin died, Jesse marched with Martin's wife, Coretta Scott King, in memory of him.

Jesse Jackson

Coretta Scott King

PEOPLE UNITED TO SERVE HUMANITY

Jesse started Operation PUSH (People United to Serve Humanity) in Chicago. His goal was to help African Americans help themselves. Every Saturday, Jesse gave a talk on TV and radio about jobs, education, and family life. His work helped increase the number of jobs open to black workers.

Many young African Americans had problems with drugs and often dropped out of school. Jesse founded PUSH-Excel in 1975. His goal was to give students hope for a better life.

LET FREEDOM RING

Students who are a part of PUSH-Excel promise to study instead of watching TV. Parents and teachers talk to each other about the students' schoolwork.

Since the 1970s, Jesse has used PUSH-Excel to help black students across the country.

THE NATIONAL RAINBOW COALITION

Social justice has always been important to Jesse. He believes all people have value. He wants those in minority groups to have the same rights and opportunities that others have. He also wants US leaders to give them more help.

In 1984, Jesse started the National Rainbow **Coalition**. He said, "Our flag is red, white, and blue, but our nation is a rainbow—red, yellow, brown, black, and white." In 1996, Jesse's two groups joined and became the Rainbow PUSH Coalition. Jesse is its president.

LET FREEDOM RING

The Rainbow PUSH Coalition helps those who are poor and hungry. The group also works for peace and **inspires** people to sign up to vote.

Jesse helps carry the Rainbow PUSH Coalition banner during a march to honor Martin Luther King Jr. in 1998.

THE CAMPAIGN FOR PRESIDENT

In 1984, Jesse became one of the first African Americans to campaign nationwide for the presidency. However, he didn't get enough votes. In 1988, he ran again. Even though he lost, he inspired others. More than 3 million new voters signed up during his campaigns.

Jesse started helping other people run for office. He asked them to pay more attention to the concerns of African American voters. Many people believe that Jesse made it possible for other African Americans to enter **politics**.

LET FREEDOM RING

Jesse still travels around the country. He tells people to vote and become active in politics.

During his presidential campaigns, Jesse often spoke about equality for minority groups.
▽

INTERNATIONAL WORK

Jesse is an **ambassador** to places all over the world. He supports the use of peaceful means to improve social equality and justice. Several times, Jesse has brought back soldiers and citizens who were prisoners in other countries.

In 1997, President Bill Clinton asked Jesse to travel to Africa. Jesse talked with African leaders about equality and freedom for all people.

In 1999, he helped get two groups in the country of Sierra Leone to sign a peace agreement.

LET FREEDOM RING

Jesse has received the Martin Luther King Jr. Nonviolent Peace Prize, the Presidential Medal of Freedom, and many other honors.

Former president Bill Clinton speaks with Jesse at a Rainbow PUSH Coalition event in 2003.

Bill Clinton

IT'S ALL IN THE FAMILY

Jesse has become a well-known face in American politics. He often comments on important issues of the day. In 2003, he spoke against the US military going into Iraq. In 2010, he wrote in favor of new health care laws.

Jesse isn't the only political voice in the Jackson family. In 1995, Jesse L. Jackson Jr. was elected to the US House of Representatives. Like his father, he worked for civil rights when he was younger.

LET FREEDOM RING

Jesse has written many books, including one he wrote with his son Jesse L. Jackson Jr.

Jesse speaks about helping poor and middle-class families in this photo from 2008.

"I AM SOMEBODY"

In the late 1960s, Jesse wrote a poem called "I Am Somebody." He has repeated it to crowds of all ages, cultures, and backgrounds. Part of the poem says, "But I am somebody. I am black, brown, white . . . I am somebody." Jesse Jackson, civil rights **crusader**, believes people of all races are important. Today, he continues to help others believe it, too.

LET FREEDOM RING

Jesse has a news show that is on the WORD cable TV network every Saturday night. Jesse also writes a weekly newspaper column.

TIMELINE

1941 — Jesse Jackson is born on October 8 in Greenville, South Carolina.

1964 — Jesse graduates from college.

1965 — Jesse joins the SCLC.

1968 — Jesse becomes a Baptist minister.

1971 — Jesse founds Operation PUSH.

1984 — Jesse founds the National Rainbow Coalition and runs for US president.

1988 — Jesse runs for president a second time.

1997 — Jesse travels to Africa for President Clinton.

GLOSSARY

ambassador: someone sent by one group or country to speak for it in different places

civil rights: the freedoms granted to US citizens by law

coalition: a group formed by joining two or more groups together

crusader: a person who fights for a cause

inspire: to cause someone to want to do something

minister: a person who leads a church service

minority group: people who are not part of the main group of a society. In the United States, African Americans, Native Americans, Latinos, and the poor are minority groups.

politician: a person who runs for or holds a government position

politics: the operations of government. A person in politics is a politician.

protest: an event at which a group objects to an idea, act, or way of doing something

FOR MORE INFORMATION

Books

Hardy, Sheila, and P. Stephen Hardy. *Extraordinary People of the Civil Rights Movement.* New York, NY: Children's Press, 2007.

Mis, Melody S. *Meet Jesse Jackson.* New York, NY: PowerKids Press, 2008.

Websites

African American Odyssey
lcweb2.loc.gov/ammem/aaohtml/
Watch videos about the history of the civil rights movement. Take a virtual trip through the exhibit at the Library of Congress.

Rainbow PUSH Coalition
www.rainbowpush.org
Get current updates about the work of the Rainbow PUSH Coalition.

Stand Up for Your Rights
pbskids.org/wayback/civilrights/
Learn more about your civil rights and the people who fought for them.

Publisher's note to educators and parents: Our editors have carefully reviewed these websites to ensure that they are suitable for students. Many websites change frequently, however, and we cannot guarantee that a site's future contents will continue to meet our high standards of quality and educational value. Be advised that students should be closely supervised whenever they access the Internet.

INDEX